pHishy
pHenomenon
A pH guide for girls.
Marcy Schaaf
English
AF483126

Welcome to the bubbly world where suds, giggles, and pH mysteries await! In "pHishy pHenomenon," we stumbles into soapy chaos, discovering that using the wrong pH balance can turn a bath into a bubbling blunder. Get ready for a hilarious adventure filled with slippery slides, hay bale hair, and a superhero's skin suit gone wrong! Until we find the secret to perfect pH, or will we be caught in the soapy shenanigans of the pHishy pHenomenon? Dive into this bubblicious tale, and let the laughter and learning begin!

understanding pH effects

Today, we learn the
magic of pH balance!

Bubble Bath Bonanza!

High pH bubbles—uh-oh! The bubbles pop,
and a not-so-sweet smell fills the air.

Lesson:

High pH smells bad!

Let's find the perfect pH for our
bubbly adventures.

Face Wash Fiasco!

Low pH face wash—oops!
Your face turns oily, like a
slippery slide!

Tip:

Low pH makes skin oily. Let's discover the ideal pH for a fresh-faced feel.

Shampoo Shenanigans!
High pH shampoo—splash!
Makes hair feels like a
hay bale!

High pH makes hair sad, Let's uncover the secret of luscious locks with perfect pH.

Bar Soap Blunder!
Low pH soap—eek!

Skin feels tight,
like a superhero's suit
gone wrong!

Let's unveil the mystery of soft,
supple skin with the right pH.

The magic number—7!
Just like tap water,
it's the skin's best friend.

Perfect pH Party!

Bubble Bash:

Our skin loves pH 7!
It's the magic number for a
bubbly, fresh, and fantastic
feeling.

Marvelous Makeover!

Use all pH 7 goodies—a bubbly bath, fresh face, silky hair, and soft skin!

Let's share the magic
of perfect pH
with our friends.

Bubbly Ballet:

Dance with us,
Feel the magic of perfect pH
and let the fun begin!

Tell the secrets of perfect pH .

What
happens with
high pH?

What soap is right for your skin?

1 2 3 4 5 6 7 8 9 10 11 12 13 14
Strongly Acidic
Weakly Acidic
Weakly Alkali
Strongly Alkali